LET'S RETHINK IT!
God's Original Plan For His Royal Children

©Sidney Sawyer III

DEDICATION

In loving memory of my sister, Sylvia Sawyer Hayes, my first proofreader and editor of my three Books before this Masterpiece of The Kingdom of God. Thank you, sister, for the love and support you always showed and the laughter and joy we experienced while in your presence.

TABLE OF CONTENTS

INSTRUCTIONS TO THE REAL YOU

The only instruction to reading this book is to understand 1 Thessalonians 5:23 *"Now may the God of peace Himself sanctify you completely; and may your whole spirit, soul, and body be preserved blameless at the coming of our Lord Jesus Christ."* Ecclesiastes 12:7 *"Then the dust will return to the earth as it was, and the spirit will return to God who gave it. When we see our loved ones in a casket, only their bodies are there; their spirits have already departed from the body at the time of death. We are a spirit, we live in a body, and we have a soul. When God looks at us, He looks at our spirit. God communicates with man through his spirit."* John 4:24 *"God is Spirit, and those who worship Him must worship in spirit and truth."*

To understand the Kingdom of Heaven, you must know the only way to enter is by your spirit. For example, when astronauts enter space, they must wear a spacesuit to survive in that atmosphere and be legal while in outer space. If the astronaut ever

LET'S RETHINK IT!

takes the spacesuit off, the laws of space will destroy the very existence of that astronaut. Even though he is in outer space, he's from the earth, exploring space in another world.

James 2:26 *"For the body without the spirit is dead, so faith without works is dead also."* The spirit inside man's body will determine that man's actions. The man inside the spacesuit controls the spacesuit's movements, actions, and directions.

John 3:1-6 *"There was a man of the Pharisees named Nicodemus, a ruler of the Jews. 2) This man came to Jesus by night and said to Him, "Rabbi, we know that You are a teacher come from God; for no one can do these signs that You do unless God is with him." 3) Jesus answered and said to him, "Most assuredly, I say to you, unless one is born again, he cannot see the kingdom of God." 4) Nicodemus said to Him, "How can a man be born when he is old? Can he enter his mother's womb a second time and be born?" 5) Jesus answered, "Most assuredly, I say to you unless one is born of water and the spirit, he cannot enter the Kingdom of God. 6) That which is born of the flesh is flesh, and that which is born of the spirit is spirit."*

You must get born again; another word for born again is to be saved or give your life to Jesus Christ. Man is a spirit who lives in a body which is also called

10

an earth suit made of dirt. This man also possesses a soul which is made up of his mind, will, emotions, and intellect. Even though this man's spirit is reborn, he must renew his soul (mind). In the book of Romans, Apostle Paul is talking to born-again people, and you will notice in the scripture he refers to them as (brethren).

Romans 12:1-2 *"I beseech you therefore, brethren, by the mercies of God, that you present your bodies a living sacrifice, holy, acceptable to God, which is your reasonable service. 2) And do not be conformed to this world, but be transformed by the renewing of your mind, that you may prove what is good and acceptable and perfect the will of God."*

This soul (mind) plays a significant role in our lives and the direction our lives will go. We can live in sin or in religion which can be a lot worse than sin, or we can understand the kingdom of God and live as kingdom citizens on this earth now. Colossians 3:2-3 *"Set your mind on things above, not on things on the earth. 3) For you died, and your life is hidden with Christ in God."* Matthew 6:33 *"But seek first the Kingdom of God and His righteousness, and all these things shall be added to you."* Do you see the writer of Colossians and Jesus saying the same thing; seek that which is above the kingdom of heaven? Colossians 3:10 *"and have put on the new man* *who is renewed in the knowledge according to the <u>image of Him</u> <u>who created him</u>."* Philippians 2:5 *"Let this mind be in you which was also in Christ Jesus."*

The word "Let" is defined as allowing or failing to prevent or permit entry. So, we can have the mind of Christ if we give it an opportunity in our life. Q: What kind of mind does Jesus Christ have while on the earth? A: He was a king; He had a Kingdom mindset. We are connected to the Kingdom of God through our born-again spirit, and our spirit is one with God. These dirt bodies we live in are just transportation for our spirit, which also makes us legal on this earth.

For example, I do this often, and you probably do it also; you see a car, and you may say, "that is Kevin," and then quickly you remember Kevin does not have that car anymore. See, you identified Kevin by the car he used to drive, and it has been seven years since Kevin had that particular vehicle. We also identify ourselves with our bodies. Does God always see the born-again spirit or the not born-again spirit of man?

We are connected to the hometown of heaven by our spirit. You must understand there are two invisible kingdoms operating on this earth simultaneously the kingdom of darkness (Satan) and the kingdom of light (God). Colossians 1:13 *"He has delivered us from the power of darkness and conveyed us into the kingdom of the Son of His love."* Matthew 12:26 *"If Satan casts out Satan, he is divided against himself. How then will his kingdom stand."* You must decide which kingdom you will choose, and both will influence your actions while on this earth.

INTRODUCTION

There's only one truth to a person's story. Are you willing to seek the truth? Are you just going to accept what you know as the truth without seeking the truth from the person himself or herself? The easiest way to find the truth is to go to the source of the truth! What was the original story? What would have caused it to change? Why did it change? Did they give up or throw in the towel from the original story? Did they just quit because it didn't work as planned? All these questions I will give you a chance to decide for yourself in this book, God's original story for His creation. You would understand His story for making man.

TERMS OF A KINGDOM

<u>King</u>- a male ruler of an independent state, especially one who inherits the position by right of birth.

<u>Kingdom</u>- a country, state, or territory ruled by a king or queen. The spiritual reign or authority of God.

<u>Will</u>- what one wishes or has determined shall be done. The purpose of God is to bless mankind through Christ. Especially His commands and precepts. Of one's will, choice, inclination, desire, and pleasure. Expressing the future tense. The faculty by which a person decides on and initiates action. Control is deliberately exerted to do something or restrain one's own impulses.

<u>Colonize</u>- of a country or its citizens, send a group of settlers to a place, and establish political control over it. To take control of (a people or area), especially as an extension of state power: to claim (someone or something) as a colony.

<u>Domain</u>- a territory owned or controlled by a ruler or government. Complete and absolute ownership of land. A territory over which dominion is

exercised. A region distinctively marked by some physical feature.
A sphere of knowledge, influence, or activity.

Dominion- sovereignty or control. The territory of a sovereign or government. Supreme authority. Domain. Absolute ownership.

Sovereignty- supreme power or authority. The authority of a state to govern itself or another state. Freedom from external control. One that is sovereign.

Citizenship- the position or status of being a citizen of a particular country.

Country- a nation with its own government occupying a particular territory. An indefinite, usually extended expanse of land—the land of a person's birth, residence, or citizenship.

Ambassador- an accredited diplomat sent by a country as its official representative to a foreign country. A person who acts as a representative or promoter of a specified activity. A diplomatic agent of the highest rank accredited to a foreign government or sovereign as the resident representative of his or her own government or sovereign or appointed for a special and often temporary diplomatic assignment. An authorized representative or messenger.

Culture- the arts and other manifestations of human intellectual achievement regarded collectively. The customs, arts, social institutions, and achievements of a particular nation, people, or other social groups. The culture of the kingdom of God

Counselor- a person trained to give guidance on personal, social, or psychological problems. A person who gives advice or counseling.

Influence- the capacity to affect the character, development, or behavior of someone or something or affect itself.

The term "kingdom of heaven" represents the place or country of heaven. The kingdom of heaven is the headquarters, the invisible kingdom, the country where the throne of God is.

The term "kingdom of God" is that country's influence on the territories. The kingdom of God is His influence.

We must establish Kingdom concepts, terms, and definitions. The Kingdom concept is the foundation of all scripture. If you don't understand, you will misinterpret the Bible. The kingdom concept is necessary for the correct interpretation and application of scripture. The kingdom concept is the main subject throughout the scriptures. The Kingdom concept provides the foundation for understanding the motivation, purpose, plans, promises, and actions of God. God is a king!! Not a President or Prime Minister.

GOD'S BIG IDEA

What was God thinking when He thought of you and I? You must know He had to be thinking Big because He is a Gigantic God! He is God, The Creator and Ruler of the universe, and the Source of all moral authority, the Supreme Being. He is also known as the King of Glory. Genesis 1:26 "And God said," so we are talking about the Gigantic God, we are talking about the Ruler of the Universe, the Supreme Being, A Superhuman being who said, *"Let us make man in Our image, after Our likeness and let them have dominion (Kingdom) over the fish of the sea, and over the fowl of the air, and the cattle, and the earth, and every creeping thing that creepeth upon the earth."* 'Likeness'- simply means humans are like God and represent God. In likeness, character, image, figure, form, shape, imagination, similarity, resemblance, and fantasy.

What was this Big God thinking? Image is a representation in the physical form, not a representation of the physical appearance. Heaven, you must understand that it is a country and a place. John describes the country of heaven in the book of Revelation 21:16 *"The city is laid out as a square; its length is as great as its breadth, and he measured the city with the reed, twelve thousand furlongs. Its length, breadth, and height are equal."* There is no way to know God without knowing what He was thinking when He made man and put him on a place called earth. We must build our case and investigate from His perspective; what was God thinking? This is how you solve mysteries.

We must think on terms like dominion, His likeness, and His image, be fruitful, multiply, replenish the earth and subdue it. We must know that God's thoughts are higher than ours. That means our thoughts must grow every day to measure what He said. We can look to Apostle Paul, Moses, King David, and all the great men who did magnificent work for the Lord! But if you are mature, you will know Jesus is our model.

He subdued every circumstance, even death itself! We must know Jesus was the perfect thought of God walking on two legs, the very thought of Genesis

1:26. Jesus quotes in John 14:9 Jesus said unto him, *"who said"? Jesus said unto him, "Have I been so long, and yet you have not known Me, Phillip? He who has seen Me has seen the Father; so how can you say, 'Show us the Father?'"* Here we see the word's image and likeness manifesting on this place called earth. Jesus was talking to one of His disciples, His close friend. See, it does not matter how close you think you are to God or Jesus if you miss their concept or idea. That is why conception is so important because misconception destroys your life.

Ask yourself what God's original idea was. Did it ever change from His original thought? You must know this concept is the key to communication. Concept (con) means to come together, (..cept) means thought. Bring them together; now that your thoughts are together, you can see a picture. That is why a misconception produces miscommunication. If you do not get my concept, you will misunderstand me. A concept is an idea, and if you miss what I am communicating to you, you will miss the whole concept. If you believe what I say and it's not true, you live your life on a lie.

Concepts are dangerous because if you believe a concept that is not true, you will be con and live on a lie for the rest of your life. Do you see why this is a great pivot point in our lives to get God's correct thoughts of Himself and us? It is extremely dangerous to have the wrong concept or idea of God. Therefore, you must ask yourself this question: do I have Christ's idea?

You can build a ministry on a misconception; a lot of people did it and are still doing it now. That is why it's important to find out what the original idea is in the mind of God (the one) who is communicating with me. Ideas are so powerful that they produce ideology, and ideologies produce your theology. Your idea is the source of your theology. Theologies produce your psychology, the way you think about things. Psychology produces your lifestyle, and you live your thoughts.

Proverbs 23:7 *"For as he thinks in his heart, so is he."* Your mentality is a source of your philosophy which comes from your Theology which comes from your ideology which comes from your ideas. I notice in our journey to please God, we miss His concept, His original intent, and His original thought of man. We focus more on the means to get us back to His original purpose of man.

When we speak of the means, let us define means — an action or system by which a result is brought about, a method. You must realize how great and powerful the blood, the cross, and the resurrection were, and they were means to get us back into God's original thought, idea, and intent for us to have dominion (kingdom). I cannot stress enough that we must know God's original idea of creation.

One thought you must look at is to extend His heavenly kingdom to earth. Jesus' disciples asked Him to teach them to pray in Matthew 6:9-10 *"In this manner, therefore, pray: Our Father in heaven, Hallowed be Your name. Your kingdom comes. Yours will be done On earth as it is in heaven."* In the scripture we just read, we can see the word "Colonize," which will be used frequently in this book. Its meaning is to send a group of settlers to (a place) and establish political control over it. God wants the earth to look and be like heaven. "Thy will be done on earth as it is in heaven!"

Let us go a little deeper. Satan tricked Adam and Eve for what God had already given them dominion (kingdom); to colonize earth as it is in heaven. You must realize they still lived on the earth, but they lost the (Holy Spirit) which gave them dominion (kingdom). We will talk about the role of the Holy Spirit later in the book.

Luke 4:5-6 *"Then the devil, taking Him up on a high mountain, showed Him all the kingdoms of the world in a moment. 6 And the devil said unto Him, "all this authority I will give You, and their glory; for this has been delivered to me, and I give it to whomever I wish."*

The serpent (devil) took the dominion, kingdom, and authority from Adam and Eve legally, and Jesus took it back legally for us. Now we must learn how to live as kingdom people who have regained their dominion, authority, and power.

HOW WE MISS THE KINGDOM

God's thoughts have always been thoughts of dominion. This word means to govern, government and governor. When you oversee something or rule it. Genesis chapter one tells you God's intent was for us to have a kingdom, not religion. We see religion has increased, and the kingdom has decreased. Jesus came back to take back what was stolen from Adam.

(Blue Clues) Let's first find who stole from Adam Genesis 3:13, "*And the LORD God said unto the woman, what is this thou hast done? And the woman said, ``the serpent (Satan) tricked me, and I did eat.*" We see that Adam and Eve were tricked, deceived, and bamboozled by the serpent or the devil. The serpent took their dominion (kingdom).

Now let's find out what they were tricked out of. Luke 4:5-6 *"Then the devil, taking Him up on a high mountain, showed Him all the kingdoms of the world in a moment of time 6) And the devil said to Him, all authority I give You and their glory; for this has been delivered to me, and I give it to whomever I wish."* We see Satan say it was given to him, but Satan did not say what he really did, which was that he deceived them. We must thank Jesus for giving us our authority, dominion, and the kingdom of God back.

Never lose God's original thought for Jesus' coming. Jesus' only message was the kingdom of God. Matthew 4:17 was the start of His ministry 17). *"From that time Jesus began to preach and to say, "repent, for the kingdom of heaven is at hand."* Jesus died a horrible death, but after His resurrection, we see death couldn't keep the message of the kingdom away.

Acts 1:3 *"To whom He also presented Himself alive after His suffering by many infallible proofs, being seen by them forty days and speaking of the things pertaining to the kingdom of God!"*

We see Jesus started the message of the kingdom, and we see Him also exiting the earth with the same message of the Kingdom of God. Six verses later, Acts 1:9 *"Now when He (Jesus) had spoken these things, while they watched, He was taken up, and a cloud received Him out of their sight."* We should see that this kingdom message should be something we seriously investigate!

Jesus told His disciples to seek first the kingdom of God Matthew 6:33. In my quest to do just that, "seek first the kingdom," my finding was that the words; king, kingdom, kings, and kingly were used over twenty-nine hundred times in the King James Version of the Bible. The only books in the Bible that doesn't use these words are very few; Ruth, Joel, Obadiah, Titus, Philemon, 1 John, 2 John, 3 John, and Jude. That's 9 books out of 66 books that make up the Bible.

So, we see the concept of God has always been a kingdom. Just look at the first words used at the creation of man; "Dominion," and the Hebrew word for dominion is Radha, meaning to reign, rule over, and have dominion. *The word "have" means -possess, own, or hold, so God said let them have dominion, possess dominion and hold dominion.* If you look at this word closely, you will see that it is a kingdom word. So, God's concept has always been kingdom when He created us. That is why Jesus' only message was the kingdom.

God's message was one the kingdom and dominion, Jesus' message was both also. John 10:30 "*My Father and I are One.*" It is impossible to have the word "kingdom" and not have the word "dominion" in its vocabulary. Words like rule, reign, and dominion make up a king and his kingdom. We must have a kingdom dominion mindset when we open the Bible to read. If we really look at it, we humans have been walking in dominion on this earth. We have taken the elements of the earth and created the cell phone, air crafts, spaceships, boats, and homes. All the elements were here on earth when Jesus, Moses, and Abraham were walking the earth to make an Airplane. To make a Jet that would break the sound barrier and allow a human to fly it is dominion.

Dominion is a mindset we have that was given to us. We have not even used the other kingdom words that God used in His creation of man. Genesis 1:28 "*Then God blessed them, and God said to them, "Be fruitful and multiply; fill the earth and subdue it.*" Subdue is the word, its meaning is to bring into subjection, bring into bondage, and keep under to conquer. Ask yourself why God used these words when describing the man. You must seek to understand what His Big Idea was; what was His concept? Was it to extend His heavenly kingdom on earth?

Jesus did say in Matthew 6:9-13 *"In this manner, therefore, pray: Our Father in heaven, Hallowed be Your name 10) Your kingdom* **comes, Yours will be done on earth as it is in heaven." Jesus said, "My Father and I are one." So, if** God thought it, Jesus is thinking it also and will also speak it. John 12:49 *"For I have not spoken on My own authority; but the Father who sent Me gave Me a command, what I should say and what I should speak."*

This is so important to know that Jesus was only saying what the father had said and saying. How many times did Jesus mention what the father was thinking when they used the word "kingdom"? It appears 53 times in 42 places in Matthew and 17 times in 13 places. In Mark, 41 times and 29 places in Luke. John only uses the phrase or words 3 times in his writings.

John 3:3 *"Jesus answered and said to him, "Most assuredly, I say to you, unless one is born again, he cannot see the kingdom of God!"* John 3:5 *Jesus answered, Most assuredly, I say to you unless one is born of water and of the spirit, he cannot enter the kingdom of God."*

John 18:36 *"Jesus answered, My Kingdom is not of this world. If My kingdom were of this world, My servants would fight, so that I should not be delivered to the Jews; but now My kingdom is not from here."*

John really emphasizes what Jesus said about the kingdom when He wrote, "Most assuredly," this meaning, in our terms in the 90s, "I swear to God," "on my grandmother," "I will put my hand on the bible," "I'm telling the truth," "man I am not lying I'm telling the truth about this kingdom stuff bro."

The word they use in 2022 is "on God" in other words, "I'm not lying!" I wonder if it is coincidental that the Bible I am reading is a King James Version. It is a king who is responsible for getting the Bible written or should I say, translated into the English language. How fitting is that? Is this really about luck or coincidence?

In 1604 King James himself, a religious scholar who had re-translated some of the Psalms, sought to unite a team to get the Bible translated into English. In 1604, England's king James authorized a new translation of the Bible aimed at settling some thorny religious differences in his kingdom.

Here we clearly see a king who has a kingdom translating the Bible I'm reading now! To really understand what we are reading, we must understand that the Bible is about a king, a kingdom, and his royal children; that is about God and His children, the human family.

I wondered when king James was re-translating some of the books of Psalms, did he get to Psalms 145: 11-13 *"They shall speak of the glory of Your kingdom, and talk of Your power, 12) To make known to the sons of men His mighty acts, and the glorious majesty of His kingdom 13) Your kingdom is an everlasting kingdom, and Your dominion endured throughout all generations. King David was here talking about the awesomeness of God, our ultimate king."*

A king talking about a king. We should be able to see through the smoke that God's Big Idea has always been dominion, kingship, and a domain to have dominion. When you look at Satan, aka Lucifer, he took dominion from Adam and Eve. If you look a little farther into the smoke, you will see Isiah 14:12 *"How are you fallen from heaven, O Lucifer, son of the morning! How are you cut down to the ground, you who weaken the nations! 13) For you have said in thine heart: I will ascend into heaven, I will exalt my throne above the stars of God: I will also sit on the mount of the congregation, on the farthest sides of the North."*

We see Lucifer (Satan) was thrown from a city called heaven. Heaven is a place where God lives and has a throne. A throne is a decorative chair used by a king, queen, or emperor on important occasions.

Lucifer (Satan) understood sitting on a throne and being a ruler. He wanted to be like God. We see so far from Jesus' perspective, Satan-Lucifer's perspective, King David's perspective, King James had a kingly perspective, and then the ultimate perspective of God. The kingdom perspective (concept) is necessary for the correct interpretation and application of the scriptures. It is the main subject throughout the scriptures and provides the foundation for understanding the motivation, purpose, plans, promises, and actions of God.

God is a King! Not a president or prime minister. I know we start at a disadvantage because we never experience living under a king.

THE AUTHOR AND FINISHER OF OUR FAITH

What does it mean to be the author and finisher of something? Hebrew 12:2 says, "*Look unto Jesus, the Author, and Finisher of our faith, who for the joy that was set before Him endured the cross, despising the shame and sat down at the right hand of the throne of God.*" I like how the NIV says it, "*fixing our eyes on Jesus, the pioneer, and perfecter of our faith.*" Message bible says, "*keep your eyes on Jesus who both began and finished this race we're in.*"

We are studying how He did it. The Greek word for the author is "archego," which means a chief leader, prince, or captain, and primarily signifies one who takes the lead in or provides the first occasion of anything. Merriam -Webster defined it as one that originates or creates something; source.

We really must explore what Jesus' mission and purpose were. His mission statement can be found in Matthew 4:17 *"Change the way you think for the kingdom of heaven is at hand."* Was Jesus talking about the people that were in His presence? Is this statement for us in 2022? The question you must answer is: will you give the correct answer? Jesus' whole focus was on the kingdom, not the cross, not the resurrection, and not being born again.

He talked about being born again once with a man named Nicodemus, who came to Him late one night, and that's the only time Jesus spoke about being born again. About His resurrection, He talked privately with His close friends, and His disciples never mentioned it to the multitudes.

The author's focus was the kingdom of God and the kingdom of heaven. We must understand how great the blood of Jesus is for the believer, how great the cross Jesus hung on, the betrayal He suffered, and God came down to this earth as a man. The resurrection was only the means, a system by which a result is achieved. A method that was used to get us into the kingdom of God. Matthew 6:33 *"But seek first the kingdom of God and His righteousness, and all these things will be added to you."*

We see that there is a priority with God, and it is the kingdom of God. If He suffered the abuse, despised the shame, and endured the cross for what, let me answer, to give us the kingdom of God? Luke 12: 31-32 *"But seek the kingdom of God, and all these things shall be added to you. 32) Do not fear little flock, for it is your father's pleasure to give you the kingdom."* Do you hear what the Father (The king say)? It's His good pleasure to give us the kingdom. The only thing Jesus asks us to seek is the kingdom of God and not just that, but His righteousness as well.

The word 'Seek' in Greek means seek for, be about, endeavor, enquire (for), require, desire, coveting earnestly, and striving after. Merriam-Webster says about to seek, to resort; go to, to go in search of, look for; to try to discover; to ask for, to try to acquire or gain; aim at.

Ask yourself, for real, have I been seeking the kingdom? Has this been my number one priority? Have I even heard about the kingdom and how to seek the kingdom? Do I know what the kingdom means? Jesus said if you seek the kingdom first, what you need will be added to you. In this book, the word kingdom will be used over a hundred times, so let's define kingdom.

A kingdom is a country, state, or territory ruled by a king or queen. A quick insert here in Alabama: when we leave to go out of the United States and go to the Bahamas or Cosmo Mexico, these are other countries outside the United States, and passports are needed. A passport is an official document issued by a government, certifying the holder's identity and citizenship and entitling them to travel under its protection to and from foreign countries.

Come go here with me quickly. Philippians 3:20-21 *"For our citizenship is in heaven; from where also we look for the savior, the Lord Jesus Christ 21) who shall change our lowly body, that it may be fashioned like unto His glorious body, according to the working whereby He is able even to subdue all things unto Himself."*

The writer of Philippians 3:20, Apostle Paul, also had dual citizenship. Acts 22:3 *"I am verily a man who is a Jew, born in Tarsus, a city in Cilicia, a region that had been made part of the Roman province of Syria by the time of Paul's adulthood."* Somehow, Paul, whose name was Saul at the time, had obtained his second citizenship from Rome.

The Roman Empire governed Israel over 2000 years ago when Paul preached the gospel. A person with Roman citizenship held high social status and received various privileges from Rome, like suffrage, the right to prosecute in court, and the right to appeal to the highest court of Rome held by the emperor. They could avoid certain punishments like whipping and crucifixion, and they did not receive the death penalty if they didn't commit treason.

Paul exercised these rights as a Roman citizen in Acts 22:22-30 *"They were about to beat Apostle Paul with a whip, but he understood his rights as a citizen."* You must understand citizenship demands rights. This is why it is so important to seek first the kingdom of God and His righteousness because, in your seeking, you will begin to understand your rights. Once you understand your rights, you pray and act differently. When we use our passports as US citizens to enter Nassau Bahamas, we are protected by the Embassy of the United States at 42 Queen St Nassau Bahamas phone number (242)322-1181.

Citizenship is powerful! As a citizen of the United States with a legal passport, we can demand protection from the US Embassy there in Nassau. But we are citizens of heaven, and we must know heaven is backing us up. Know your rights that Jesus paid for!

What is an embassy? It is the headquarters for US Government representatives serving in a foreign country. Inside the US Embassy in Nassau Bahamas, it's normally led by an ambassador, who is the US president's representative to the host country. An embassy is normally located in the capital city. The Bible tells us that we are ambassadors for Christ, the anointed one (king), not the president. 2 Corinthians 5:20 *"Now then we are ambassadors for Christ, as though God did beg you by us; we pray you in Christ's stead be ye reconciled (to restore to friendship or harmony) to God."*

An ambassador represents a country good, do you get it? We represent the country called heaven. This lines up with the prayer Jesus told His disciples to pray when they asked Him to teach them how to pray Matthew 6:9-10 *"After this manner, therefore, pray ye; Our Father which is in Heaven, hallowed be thy name. 10) Thy kingdom come; thy will be done in earth as it is in heaven."* God wants what's going on in heaven to be going on in earth. That's the father's will now, the same as it was with Adam.

We must know God's original intent for man and earth. Mogadishu, Somalia, is a third-world country that has a United States of America Embassy. Even though it's a third-world country, it doesn't affect the US Embassy there because the United States provides for all their embassy, not for them to be eating beans and rice in Somalia but in the embassy, they are eating crab legs, crawfish, ribeye steak, why because the United States is their source, so the ambassador is good.

Heaven wants to be our supply chain as kings, citizens, and ambassadors from the home country of heaven.

KING DOMAIN

According to Genesis, the whole universe is God's domain by creation rights. God did not have to fight for territory. King David said in Psalms 24:1 *"The earth is the Lord's and everything in it."* The world and all its people belong to Him by creation rights. Colossians 1:16 *"For by Him all things were created that are in heaven and that are on earth, visible and invisible, whether thrones or dominions or rulers or principalities or power. All things were created through Him and for Him."*

Psalms 115:16 says, "The heaven, even the heavens, are the Lord's but the earth He has given to the children of men." We must understand that there is no chaos in heaven, the chaos is in the earth, and Jesus came to set order back in the earth. Now it is up to us to conquer territory to manifest the Kingdom of God and bring the influence of heaven throughout the earth.

A king-domain which is why it is called a kingdom, and it's simply a king ruling a domain. David, the son of Jessie, did an excellent job running his domain. When they say David, the son of Jessie, this is him that was overlooked. He was the youngest of eight boys who attended to the sheep and was the errand boy.

When Prophet Samuel came to Jessie, David's father's house, to anoint the next king over Israel, 1 Samuel 16:5 *"And he said, peaceably I am come to sacrifice to the Lord; sanctify yourselves and come with me to the sacrifice. Then he consecrated Jesse and his sons and invited them to the sacrifice 6) So when they came, he looked at Eliab and said, "Surely the Lord's anointed is before him!" 7) The Lord said to Samuel, "Do not look at his appearance or physical stature because I have refused him. For the Lord does not see as man sees, for man looks at the outward appearance, but the Lord looks at the heart."*

Verse 8 "Then Jesse called Abinadab and made him pass before Samuel, and he said, neither hath the Lord has chosen him." A commercial break from scripture; breaking news, no matter who looked down on you because of your appearance, where you come from, what you have or may not have, whatever the case might be about your past failure, know this, Ephesian 1:4 *"Just as He chose us in Him before the foundation of the world, that we should be Holy and without blame before Him in love."* This is great news, people of God. You have been chosen by God. If you were not invited to the ceremony, just wait God will let you make your grand entrance so everybody can see you coming. It is a setup for kingship.

During the commercial break, we see the first pick was by Prophet Samuel, who favored Eliab. The second pick was by David's father Jessie, and his choice was Abinadab. Jesse third picked Shamah. Verse 10 *"Again Jesse made seven of his sons to pass before Samuel and Samuel said unto Jesse the Lord hath not chosen these."*

Here we see the fourth, fifth, sixth, and seventh picks. And the King draft looks like it is over. God had a draft before there was an NBA, NFL, or MLB draft. We see in 1 Samuel 16:1, *"Now the Lord said to Samuel how long will you mourn for Saul seeing I have rejected him from reigning over Israel?"* Let's take a quick detour to find out how Saul even became king. The story is found in 1 Samuel 8:5-7 *"They said to him, (Samuel) "you are old, and your sons do not walk in your ways; now appoint a king to lead us, such as all the other nations have." 6 But when they said, "give us a king to lead us, "this displeased Samuel; so he prayed to the LORD. 7, And the LORD told him: "listen to all that the people are saying to you; it is not you that they have rejected, but they have rejected Me as their King."*

God wanted to be their king, but the people chose Saul to be their king instead of God because of how he looked. They wanted a King that looked like he could be a king, a king they could see as the rest of the nations had. Now we see God choosing a king for them, *"Fill your horn with oil and go. I am sending you to Jesse the Bethlehemite, for I have provided Myself a king among his sons."* Now we see where the draft pick originated from because God could have very well said go to Jesse's house and anoint David as king. Yes, He could have been more specific.

See, it really does not matter when you get picked. It is what you do when you get picked. Tom Brady was the 199 pick out of 259 players. Could you imagine you enter the NFL draft and the 5-time MVP player and 7-time super bowl champion, watching 198 players go before him, my God! The thing about David, he was the last pick in the king's draft but wasn't invited. He didn't have to experience the agony and frustration Tom Brady had to experience watching the draft, and he left the house at one time, his father had to come outside to comfort him because he became very disappointed.

And David went on to be a Great king. King David did a great job with the other men that were picked last. 1 Samuel 22:1 *"David, therefore, departed from there and escaped to the cave Adullam. So when his brethren and all his father's house heard it, they went down there to him. 2) And everyone who was in distress, everyone who was in debt, and everyone who was discontented, gathered themselves to him. So he became captain over them. And there were about four hundred men with him."*

You must realize when you put the king in front of David's name, it means he is responsible for his domain to rule it, subdue it, and reign. And that is what David, or should I say King David did when he took 400 men that were at rock bottom. They took on his spirit and kingdom mentality. 37 of the men were called King David's mighty men. Their story is found in 2 Samuel 23:8-39 *"These are the names of the mighty men whom David had: Josheb-Basshebeth the Tachmonite, chief among the captains. He was called Adino the Senate; because he had killed eight hundred men at one time. And after him was Eleazar, he arose and smote the Philistines until his hand was weary and his hand clung unto the sword, and the Lord wrought a great victory that day.*

After he was Shammah, he stood in the midst of the field and defended the ground full of lentils after everyone fled from the Philistines, he slew the Philistines, and the Lord wrought a great victory. And 3 of the 30 chief went down and came to David in the harvest time unto the cave of Adullam and the troop of the Philistines encamped in the valley of Rephaim and David long for a drink of water from the well in Bethlehem and the three mighty men brake through the host of the Philistines and drew water out of the well of Bethlehem David did not drink the water because they risk their life to get the water. David pours it out to the Lord. Abisha, lifted up his spear against three hundred and slew them. Benaiah, slew two lionlike men; he also went down into a pit in the snow and killed a lion. And he slew an Egyptian, an impressive man, and the Egyptian had a spear in his hand, but he went down to him with a staff and plucked the spear out of the Egyptian hand and slew him with his own spear. This sounds like when David cut Goliath's head off with his own sword."

The Bible identified these men as let us go back to 1 Samuel 22:2 "*And everyone who was in distress; everyone who was in debt, and everyone who was discontented gathered to him. So he (David) became captain over them. And there were about four hundred men with him.*" These were ordinary men that experienced life just as we do in 2022; in debt, bitter about life, with no direction for their life, and in distress. Sounds like I was once upon a time in my life.

And with king David as their captain, they became courageous with a vision just like their leader. This is the same thing that happened when Jesus took ordinary men who had experienced highs and lows in life. They became courageous like their leader and teacher, Jesus.

Let us take the Boston Patriots, founded in 1959; for instance, the name was changed in 1971 to the New England Patriots, and they had not won a super bowl in 40 years until Tom Brady became a captain, a leader who was passed by 198 draft picks. Ask yourself, who passed me by? Who overlooked me? You must remind yourself that God has chosen you in Him before the foundation of the earth.

Do you really understand what the word of God has said? I picked you before the earth existed. The one thing you must understand is that there is something God cannot do. Yes, there is something God cannot do, and there is something you cannot do, so do not judge God because He cannot lie! If He said it, it is true and cannot be taken back. Genesis 1:26 *"Then God said, "Let Us make man in Our image, according to Our likeness; let them have dominion verse 28 Then God blessed them, and God said to them, "Be fruitful and multiply; fill the earth and subdue it; have dominion."*

The word dominion comes from the word domain; God's original intent is for us to have dominion over our domain. Ezra J. Warner created or invented the can opener on January 5, 1858, and its purpose was to open tin cans. It really did not matter if you understood how it worked. It did not matter if you used it for something else. The reason the purpose and original intent of Ezra J. Warner never changed is because you did not know its original intent. This is the exact same way with our creator, His intent and purpose for man never ever changed from Genesis 1; dominion (Kingdom)!

WHAT'S THE WILL

1 John 5:14-15 *"Now this is the confidence that we have In Him, that if we ask anything according to His will, He hears us. And if we know that He hears us, whatever we ask, we know that we have the petitions that we have asked of Him."*

It is imperative that we know what God's will is so we can get it done on earth as it is in the country of heaven. Jesus' disciples asked Him to "teach us to pray." Matthew 6:9-10 *"In this manner, therefore, pray: Our Father in Heaven, hallowed be Your name. Your kingdom come. Yours will be done on earth as it is in heaven."* In teaching His disciples how to pray, in the process, Jesus is teaching how to manifest the will of God.

John writes, "if you ask anything according to His will, know that He Hears you, and you can have it." In saying "Our Father," this is a very intimate statement that indicates we are not just saying words in the air. But we are speaking directly to Our Father (Daddy), who chose us to do His will. If Symone MeKayla Sawyer or Sidney Sawyer IV ask of me anything according to my will, for them, it's done now. See, you can have your own will different from the will of your father.

Jesus came down from a country called heaven to do his father's will, to teach and show us how His will should be done on earth. John 6:37-40 *"All that the Father gives Me will come to Me, and the one who comes to Me I certainly will not cast out. For I have come down from heaven, not to do My own will, but the will of the one who sent Me. And this is the will of the father who sent Me, that of all He has given Me, I shall lose none but raise it up on the last day. And this is the will of the one who sent Me, that everyone who sees the Son and believes in Him shall have everlasting life; and I will raise him on the last day."*

John 4:34 "Jesus said to them, *"My food is to do the will of Him who sent Me and to accomplish His work."* Jesus was very serious about doing the will of the father, and we should also be. Jesus was the perfect example of God's will on earth, not Apostle Paul, Apostle Peter, Apostle John, or King David. Is your pastor, mother, father, or Donald Trump your example of doing the will of the father? King David was a highly successful king because his desire was to do the will of God, our father. Psalms 143:10 *"Teach me to do Your will, for You are my God: Your Spirit is good. Lead me in the land of uprightness."*

Ask yourself these few questions, if you will, and take the time to answer correctly. Do I know what Father God's will is? Has His will changed in Genesis 1:26 *"Then God said, 'Let Us make man in Our image, according to Our likeness; let them have dominion (Kingdom) over the fish in the sea, the fowl in the air, the cattle, and over all the earth, and every creeping thing that creeps on the earth."* Ask yourself this question also, has God's will changed in Genesis 1:28 *"Then God blessed them, and God said to them, 'Be fruitful, and multiply, and replenish the earth, and subdue it; have dominion (Kingdom) over the fish of the sea, and over every living thing that moves on the earth."?*

If someone dies and they are resurrected, will they return to their formal state of being? Let us establish that Jesus came to restore (resurrect) man back to the position Adam lost. We have been resurrected back to the place Adam was before the fall. We are back on top of the mountain. We have been made the righteousness of God in Christ Jesus. Thank you, Lord!

It would be important to break down the argument Apostle Paul was having in 1 Corinthians 15, Apostle Paul argues the facts about the resurrection of Christ, also the parallel between Jesus and Adam, and the differences between the two as well. 1 Corinthians 15:22 *"For as in Adam all die, even so in Christ shall all be made alive."*

Apostle Paul was writing to individuals in Corinth that were teaching there was no resurrection of the dead. He testified to the church members in Corinth that Jesus rose from the dead. Let's investigate the argument in 1 Corinthians 15:12-14 *"Now if Christ is preached that He rose from the dead, how say some among you that there is no resurrection of the dead? 13) But if there be no resurrection of the dead, then is Christ not risen: 14) And if Christ does not rise, then is our preaching worthless, and your faith is also worthless."* Verse 22 *"For as in Adam all die, even so in Christ shall all be made alive."*

Remember Christ means the Messiah or the Anointed King; know this because in verse 24, Apostle Paul shifts into the Kingdom of God. 1 Corinthians 15:24 *"Then comes to an end when He delivers the Kingdom to God the Father when He puts an end to all rule and all authority and power. 25) For He must reign till He has put all enemies under His feet. 26) The last enemy that He will be destroyed is death. We come full circle to God's original will."* verse 25 *"For He must reign, who must reign (rule) Jesus Christ the King of the kingdom of God."*

Let us take another approach to this whole situation using a parable. There is a girl 13 years of age who is a promising tennis player. Her father is a master Plummer started up his company, Mobile Plumbing Incorporation. Her father has been training his daughter since birth to be the world's number 1 player: the Grand Slam Tennis Champion. Number 1 in Wimbledon, US Open, Australian Open, and French Open. After a long day at work, the father arrives home and notices the house is engulfed with flames, almost burned completely, but it does not stop the father from rushing into the home, knowing his daughter is asleep. Not for one second was he concerned for his own life. The father saved his daughter's life. And he sustained 85 % third-degree burns. In his successful quest to save his daughter, who suffered no burn damage, only the father was burnt. After spending three days in ICU in a coma, the father awakens, asking where his daughter is. After 12 months of recovery, the father's business, Mobile Plumbing Incorporation, begins to flourish, and his daughter continues to dominate on the tennis court. Even though the daughter was incredibly grateful for her father risking his life for her, she will never forget the love her father showed by his actions to rescue her.

The father's will, purpose, and plans never changed for his daughter, and her love for tennis even increased. They frequently look back on what happened and celebrate life and love!

We should never forget what Jesus Christ did; He died for us so that we might live for Him and fulfill the father's will for our life. The father's plan for us before birth was Genesis 1:26-28. We were created in His Image and likeness, so God knows our capabilities. Verse 28 is a kingdom mandate to God's Royal Children, *"Then God blessed them, and God said to them, be fruitful and multiply; fill the earth and subdue it; have dominion."* (Kingdom)! Because Jesus went through the fire of the cross and death, His original purpose (will) never changed because a falling angel had tricked us in Genesis 1 for our Dominion (Kingdom).

UNDERSTANDING THE SOURCE OF THE INVISIBLE

In Psalms 24:1, King David starts off: *"The earth is the Lord and the fullness thereof; the world, and they that dwell therein."* We must understand God is the creator and the source of our living. He created air, oxygen, and other elements you cannot see with the visible eye, such as the Kingdom of God, but you can see the effects of the invisible. Jesus was explaining the Kingdom of God to Nicodemus, a ruler of the Jews and a master teacher.

The Message Bible John 3:5-8 *"Jesus said,"* You're not listening. Let Me say it again. Unless a person submits to this original creation, the wind-hovering-over-the-water creation, the invisible moving the visible, a baptism into a new life-it's not possible to enter God's Kingdom. When you look at a baby, it's a body you can look at and touch. But the person who takes shape within is formed by something you can't see, *and touch the Spirit and becomes a living spirit. So don't be so surprised when I tell you that you must be 'born from above- out of this world, so to speak. You know well enough how the wind blows this way and that. You hear it rustling through the trees, but you have no idea where it comes from or where it's headed next. That's the way it is with everyone 'born from above by the wind of God, the Spirit of God."*

In Jesus' conversation with Nicodemus, He explains to him if you really do not understand the things you see, how can you understand the things you cannot see, such as the wind where it blows, where is it going? We do not understand our need for oxygen until we need it. Oxygen is our source of living on earth. Oxygen is defined as a colorless, odorless reactive gas, the chemical element of atomic number 8, and the lifesupporting component of the air. If breathing stops, no oxygen gets to the brain, and the cells begin to die.

In this book, you see our source of living, the way God designed us to live. We must embrace the invisible Kingdom of God. You must understand the Kingdom of God is 0% religious! This is our source for living God's life. The Kingdom we must seek to understand the system of the Kingdom of God! Out of all the things, peoples, and places in this world, you must ask yourself why God said, "Seek first" make this your number one priority, "the kingdom of God."

You need to understand in your seeking the Kingdom, there is a source you tab into, where things will be added to you. What things you may ask, everything you need, and God knows what you need, and He can get it to you without you working two jobs.

Matthew 6:33 *"But seek ye first the kingdom of God, and His Righteousness, and all these things shall be added unto you."* Wisdom for your marriage, financial wisdom, healing for your body and mind, restoration for your family, food, forgiveness, and, my favorite, you get your identity back. Could I make a bold statement? We are a nation of ignored kings. We absolutely do not know who we are! God has given us dominion, which means Kingdom, and most of us have no clue about our kingly identity! Just as King David dominated his territory and taught others how to dominate also, Jesus dominated His territory and taught others also!

The Kingdom of God is meant to be advancing in our generation. When a king conquers a territory, he sends a Governor to that territory and converts the people there into its culture. One of the first things that would get change is the people's language and lifestyle because they are under new management. The Governor that is sent is the King's right-hand man. He has the heart of the King. The Governor would be totally responsible for converting the conquered land to resemble the homeland where the King resides. This is called colonizing, where you take a group of settlers to (a place) and establish political control over it.

The Governor's assignment is to make sure that the people in the colony do not learn their history but learn the history of the Kingdom of God. Our history is sin, corruption, and death. But when you learn the history of the Kingdom of God, it is life, eternal life, savior, and redeemer. The King says to study that history so you can say that all the citizens that are in Christ's Kingdom are called a new creation.

The Holy Spirit is the Governor of the Kingdom of God. King Jesus made the statement, *"I must go so that the Holy Spirit, the comforter can come, and He will lead you to all truth."* The only way to understand the Holy Spirit, who is the Governor is to understand the Kingdom. You must understand that when Adam and Eve fell, they lost the Holy Spirit. He is called the Holy Spirit because He's Holy. He dwells in Holy bodies, not the sinful ones, unrighteous bodies.

If you were there to see Adam and Eve before and after the fall, there would be no difference in their appearance, it looked like nothing ever happened. But the worst that could ever happen happened; they lost the Holy Spirit. So when Eve and Adam ate from the forbidding tree, sin entered, and the Holy Spirit departed.

King Jesus' purpose for coming to earth was to reintroduce the Kingdom of God and to make us Righteous, to restore the Holy Spirit to dwell in the believers, the citizens of the Kingdom of God. The Holy Spirit knows everything; I mean everything about the Kingdom of Heaven or, should I say, the country of Heaven. Heaven is the country we are from; we were just sent to earth to colonize it. God extended the country of Heaven to earth.

Ephesians 1:4 *"Just as He chose us in Him before the foundation of the world, that we should be holy and without blame before Him in love. If we were chosen before the foundation of the world, that means we were with Him."*

Ask yourself where He was, He was in a country called Heaven. If we were in Him before He created the earth, we were in the hometown of Heaven also. When my wife was carrying my son Sidney Sawyer IV, she was in the state of Alabama even though my son was not born yet, he was already in Alabama because he was in his mother's womb. We created a little earth for him, decorated his room and painted it blue, added a baby bed, put pictures on the wall, and had baby monitors so we could observe what he was doing when we were not in the room.

The Holy Spirit wants to show us His expertise in the things of Heaven and earth, He knows it all. Jesus calls the Holy Spirit, our Helper in John 14:16-17 *"And I will pray for the Father, and He will give you another Helper, that He may be with you forever; the Spirit of truth, whom the world cannot receive because it neither sees Him nor knows Him, but you know Him, for He dwells with you and will be in you."*

John 16:7 *"Nevertheless I tell you the truth. It is to your advantage that I go away; for if I do not go away, the Helper will not come to you; but if I go, I will send Him to you."*

Let us define the word 'Helper.' In Greek, it is called "Parakletos," meaning an intercessor, counselor, advocate, and comforter. Parakletos is the one summoned, called to one's aid, and is used of. (1) Christ is in His exaltation at God's right hand, pleading with God the Father for the pardon of our sins (1 Jn 2:1); and (2) the Holy Spirit destined to take the place of Christ with the apostles (after Christ's ascension to the Father), to lead them to a deeper knowledge of the gospel truth, and give them divine strength needed to enable them to undergo trials and persecutions on behalf of the divine Kingdom.

This comes from the New Strong's Concordance, the role and purpose of the Holy Spirit AKA the Helper, the Counselor, the Advocate, and the Spirit of Truth. Even though Jesus taught the Kingdom of God for three years while on earth, Jesus still prayed to the Father to send the Holy Spirit to continue to teach us about the Kingdom of God. John 16:13 *"However, when He, the Spirit of Truth, has come. He will guide you into all truth; for He will not speak on His own authority, but whatever He hears He will speak; and He will tell you things to come."*

The role of the Holy Spirit (Governor of the Kingdom) was to come to live with the citizens of the Kingdom of God once King Jesus left the earth to return to Heaven's hometown. John 14:26 *"But the Comforter, which is the Holy Spirit, whom the Father will send in My Name, He shall teach you all things, and bring all things to your remembrance, whatsoever I have said unto you."* We see whatever Jesus had taught, the Holy Spirit would continue to teach and bring to our remembrance what Jesus had already taught us about the Kingdom.

John 15:26-27 *"But when the Comforter comes, whom I will send unto you from the Father, even the Spirit of truth, which proceeded from the Father, He shall testify of Me. 27 And ye also shall bear witness, because ye have been with Me from the beginning."*

We see the entrance of the Holy Spirit in Acts 2:4 *"And they were filled with the Holy Spirit and began to speak with other languages, as the Spirit gave them utterance."* In the chapter before we see the Holy Spirit coming and Jesus exiting. Acts 1:8-11 *"But ye shall receive power, after that the Holy Spirit is come upon you: and ye shall be witnesses unto Me both in Jerusalem, and in all Judaea, and in Samaria, and unto the uttermost part of the earth. 9 And when He had spoken these things, while they looked, He was taken up; and a cloud received Him out of their sight 10 And while they looked steadfastly towards Heaven as He went up, behold, two men stood by them in white apparel; 11 Which also said, Ye men of Galilee, why stand ye gazing up into*

Heaven? This same Jesus, which is taken up from you into Heaven, shall so come in like manner as ye have seen Him go into Heaven."

We see that when the Holy Spirit came, He first messed with their language. When a king conquered territory; once he leaves to return to his home country, he sends a governor to colonize the people. The first step was to change the language of the people so they could understand what the King wanted.

Galatians 4:4 *"But when the fullness of time came, God sent forth His Son, born of a woman, born under the law."*

When Jesus came to earth, the Roman Empire ruled the world. They were colonizing every territory they militarily conquered. So, any place you went to that the Romans conquered looked like Rome and the people spoke the same language as the Romans. This is what you call being colonized. The King of Rome's purpose was to conquer and convert the whole world to Romans. This was the same mission statement Jesus had. This was a perfect time for Jesus to come because the people had a picture of a kingdom that colonized them.

The disciples could understand the prayer, our Father, which art in the Country of Heaven, let your will be done on earth as it is in the Country of Heaven. In other words, colonize us, Lord. It was not always like this in the Old Testament when kings conquered territory, they killed everybody and everything. 1 Samuel 15:1-3 *"One day, Samuel also said to Saul, "The Lord told me to choose you to be King over His people, over Israel. Now listen to this message from the Lord. 2" When the Israelites were on their way out of Egypt, the nation of Amalek attacked them. I am the Lord All-Powerful, and now I will make Amalek pay! 3 "Go and attack the Amalekites! Destroy them and all their possessions. Don't have any pity, kill their men, women, children, and even babies. Slaughter their cattle, sheep, camels, and donkeys."*

We see God was not always about colonizing. We also see where Pharoah made the Hebrews slaves in Egypt when he became ruler of that territory.

IT'S FOR YOU TO KNOW THE MYSTERY OF THE KINGDOM

Jesus told His disciples it is for you to know the mysteries of the Kingdom of Heaven. Let us get this word out the way. "Mysteries" is from the Greek word "Musterion," which means outside the range of unassisted natural apprehension and can be made known only by divine revelation.

And is made known in a manner and at a time appointed by God and to those only who are illumined by His Spirit.

In an ordinary sense, a mystery implies knowledge withheld. Colossians 1:26 *"The mystery that has been hidden for ages and generation, but now has been revealed to His saints."* Matthew 13:11 *"He answered and said to them, "because it has been given to you to know the mysteries (secret) of the Kingdom of Heaven, but to them, it has not been given.*" There are mysteries God is revealing to us today in 2022.

Also, let us read this same scripture from the Message Bible, *"He replied, you've been given insight into God's Kingdom; you know how it works. Not everybody has this gift, this insight; it hasn't been given to them."*

Whenever someone has a ready heart for this, insight and understanding flow freely. But if there is no readiness, any trace of receptivity soon disappears. The Kingdom has secrets that make the kingdom work for you.

Matthew 16:19 *"And I will give you the keys of the kingdom of heaven: and whatever you bind on earth will be bound in heaven: and whatever you loose on earth will be loosed in heaven."* So, you can have keys, but you need to know what doors they lock and unlock. This means you can be in the Kingdom and starve because you do not know the keys to the Kingdom of God.

We see Jesus has been teaching His disciples' deep secrets about the Kingdom of Heaven. When you talk of a kingdom, you must mention power and authority. We admit that the disciples had the best teacher to teach them about the Kingdom; the King of Kings and the creator of the Kingdom. In the earlier chapter, we talked about Ezra creating the can opener that no one could explain better than Ezra. Jesus specialized in this teaching; he was an expert. He invented the system.

Let's see if His disciples learned well. We would look at before and after the resurrection of Jesus Christ. First, Matthew 10:1 *"And when He had called unto Him His twelve disciples. He gave them power against unclean spirits, cast them out, and healed all manner of sickness and disease."*

Mark 6:7 *"And He called the twelve to Himself and began to send them out two by two and gave them power over unclean spirits."*

Luke 10:9 *"And heal the sick there, and say to them, 'The Kingdom of God has come near to you."*

Luke 10:17 *"Then the seventy returned with joy, saying, "Lord, even the demons are subject to us in Your name."*

Post-resurrection, Jesus arose and sat down at the right hand of the Father. Acts 2:43 *"Then fear came upon every soul, and many wonders and signs were done through the Apostles."* Acts 5:12-16 *"And through hands of the Apostles, many signs and wonders were done among the people. And they were all with one accord in Solomon's Porch. Yet none of the rest dared to join them, but the people esteemed them highly. And believers were increasingly added to the Lord, multitudes of both men and women, so that they brought the sick out into the streets and laid them on beds and couches so that at least the shadow of Peter passing by might fall on some of them. Also, a multitude gathered from surrounding cities to Jerusalem, bringing sick people and those who were tormented by unclean spirits, and they were all healed."*

These disciples had no idea about the Kingdom of God and His power until they were taught by their Master and Teacher, Jesus. You must really understand that a disciple is a follower or student of a teacher, leader, or philosopher. You must realize that a good student will become like their teacher and eventually better. Jesus was these guys' teacher, and we see in the scripture how they were doing what Jesus taught them.

What was Jesus' doctrine (teaching) you should most definitely know by now? The Kingdom of God! In Mark 1:22 *"And they were astonished at His teaching, for He taught them as one having authority, and not as the scribes."* Verse 27 *"Then they were all amazed, so that they questioned among themselves, saying, "what thing is this? What new doctrine (teaching) is this? For with authority, He commands even the unclean spirits, and they do obey Him."*

This is the teaching the disciples were under for three years. Even though the disciples lived in a kingdom, it took them a while to understand the Kingdom Jesus was bringing them to but thank God, they got the understanding. The same teaching is still available for those who will repent and receive the Kingdom and enter it.

How did we get off the yellow brick road, Dorothy? How? When Jesus was very pacific as you go proclaimed this message, *"The Kingdom of Heaven has come near."* What message? This is the message of the Kingdom! Ask yourself when was the last time you heard this message of the Kingdom of God. Please take time to answer the question. I will wait for you! This message will make you excited about being a Kingdom citizen and follower of Jesus Christ.

At least four of the disciples, James, Peter, Andrew, and John, were fishermen, while Matthew was a tax collector. So little do we know about the rest of the disciples? It's great to know they were ordinary men that received the teaching of the Kingdom of God and turned the world upside down. This let me know I can turn the world upside also because the Kingdom has come and is here.

The Apostles amazed the people like their teacher, Jesus Christ. Acts 3:1-11 *"Now Peter and John went up together to the temple at the hour of prayer, the ninth hour. 2) And a certain man lame from his mother's womb was carried, whom they laid daily at the gate of the temple which is called Beautiful, to ask alms (beg for donation) from those who entered into the temple; 3) who, seeing Peter and John about to go into the temple, ask for alms. 4) And fixing his eyes on him, Peter, with John, Peter said, "look on us." 5) So he gave them his attention, expecting to receive something from them. 6) Then Peter said, silver and gold have I none; but what I do have I give you: In the Name of Jesus Christ of Nazareth, rise up and walk. 7) And he took him by the right hand and lifted him up, and immediately his feet and ankle bones received strength. 8) So he, leaping up, stood and walked and entered the temple with them- walking and praising God. 9) And all the people saw him walking and praising God. 10) Then they knew that it was he who sat begging alms at the Beautiful Gate of the temple, and they were filled with wonder and amazement at what had happened to him. And as the lame man which was healed held Peter and John, all the people ran together unto them in the porch called Solomon's greatly wondering."* We see here that the people were in amazement at the power of the apostles.

JESUS ONLY MESSAGE FOR 3 YEARS

Jesus could waste no time, he had only three years to complete what he came to do. In the scripture, we see Jesus was not wasteful after he had fed the five thousand, not including women and children. You know more women and children come to church than men, so it could have been easily over fifteen thousand people there. There was a little boy there, we know it was his lunch Jesus multiplied, so we know it was not a men's conference.

If you look at John 6:12, "*When they were filled, He said unto His disciples, gather up the pieces that remain, that nothing be lost.*" In another place, Jesus was very precise and detailed after He was beaten, crucified, horribly treated, hung on a cross, and put in a tomb. Verse 7 of John 20 says, "*And the napkin, that was about His head, not lying with the linen clothes but wrapped together in a place by itself.*" The Message bible said, "*Neatly folded by itself.*" Bible takes a whole verse to tell us how neatly it was folded. Jesus was highly organized and detailed. And His Father was the same way.

Exodus 25:1 *"And the LORD spake unto Moses saying. 2) speak unto the children of Israel that they bring Me an offering: of every man that giveth it willingly with his heart ye shall take My offering. The offering was for the making of God's tabernacle."* We see the details of making the tabernacle in Exodus chapters 25, 26, and 27.

Exodus 25:8 *"Let them make Me a sanctuary that I may dwell among them. 9) according to all that I show thee after the pattern of the tabernacle, and the pattern of all the utensils, furniture, and even so, shall ye make it."*

Exodus 26:7 *"And thou shalt make curtains of goat hair to be a covering upon the tabernacle eleven curtains shalt thou make."*

Exodus 27:10 *"And the twenty pillars thereof and their twenty sockets shall be of brass; the hooks of the pillars and their fillets shall be of silver."*

We see that our Father-God is very detailed. It took Him three long chapters to give the details of His tabernacle. The Father and the son for sure know what they want and how they want it, and that is for sure. Jesus was very pacific when He told His disciple what to preach in Matthew 10:7 *"As you go, proclaim this message; The kingdom of Heaven has come."* (NIV).

Let us define 'This' 1) it is used to identify a specific person or thing close at hand or being indicated or experienced, 2) referring to a specific thing or situation just mentioned. The first introduction of the Kingdom by Jesus is found in Matthew 4:17 *"From that time Jesus began to preach and to say repent (change the way you think) for the kingdom of heaven is at hand (near)." And Jesus also knew we would change the message to something good that would not be this message of the Kingdom.*

You had to change how you thought 2000 years ago to receive and understand the Kingdom, and today you must change how you think (repent) to accept and understand the Kingdom of Heaven. The word 'Repent' in Greek is "Metanoeo," meaning to think differently or afterward. Reconsider, to perceive, the mind, the seat of moral reflection, to perceive beforehand. To change one's mind or purpose.

We must be attentive to every word Jesus say because if not, we will get our own concept and miss His concept. Some people will say Jesus preached the Kingdom before His crucifixion, and they are truly right. Also, He taught it after His resurrection. Let me show you Acts 1:3 *"To whom also He showed Himself alive after His passion (suffering) by many infallible proofs, being seen of them forty days and speaking of things about the kingdom of God."*

The word 'Pertaining' is the word "Peri" in Greek. It means through (all over) with respect to; use in various applications of place, cause, or time. Of, for, concerning, about, above, against, at, on, and on behalf of. How it will go.

So, the word pertaining covers everything about the Kingdom of God. You really must understand Jesus' disciples lived in a kingdom under a king, so they understood the concept and what Jesus was saying about His Kingdom. So, in this western world we live in, we have no concept of a king and his Kingdom, and we read the bible from our western mindset.

In 1776 some English men rebelled against King George III on the day that we now celebrate as Independence Day, also known as the 4TH of July. So, the United States was built on the rebellion of a group of English men who rebelled against the King.

Therefore, our concept of understanding a kingdom system is not there until we first seek the Kingdom of God. Do we truly understand when Jesus says to seek first, it means this should be our priority? Not the blood, not the cross, not the resurrection first, but the Kingdom. The Kingdom existed before the cross, before the resurrection.

We must have the cross, the blood, and the resurrection to enter the Kingdom and the born-again experience. Now, what is after being born again and getting filled with the Holy Spirit, which is the Governor of the Kingdom of God? Do we stay at the cross? No! We explore the Kingdom! *"Seek first the kingdom of God and His righteousness, and all these things will be added to you."* Matthew 6:33. What things will be added to me? Everything I need.

There's also that group that says Apostle Paul did not preach the Kingdom of God. That is a good point, I'm glad you brought it up. Paul wrote correction letters and encouraging letters to all the churches to the Philippians, Ephesians, Colossians, and Philemon, Paul's prison epistles (the epistles are letters written to the fledgling churches and individual believers in the earliest days of Christianity). Apostle Paul wrote the first 13 of these letters, each addressing a specific situation or problem. So you can't equate this with Paul didn't preach the Kingdom of God.

Apostle Paul encourages the Thessalonian church to stand strong in the face of strong persecution. In the church in Corinthians, Paul corrects and comforts. The church in Galatians warns them we are not saved by obeying the law but by faith in Jesus Christ. It tells us in Acts 28:30-31 Before all the encouragement and correction to the churches verse 30) "*And Paul dwelt two whole years in his hired house and received all that came unto him 31) preaching the kingdom of God and teaching those things which concern the Lord Jesus Christ with all confidence, no man forbidding him.*"

You must understand a lot of confusion entered the church when the Kingdom of God was preached. Jesus let us know that when the Kingdom of God is preached, Satan comes immediately to steal the word. Matthew 13:19 "*When anyone heareth the word of the kingdom and understand it not then cometh Satan and catches away that which was sown in his heart.*"

This is he which received seed by the wayside. Satan himself comes when this word of the Kingdom is preached.

JESUS AND THE FATHER ARE ONE

God establishes His purpose at the beginning with words like dominion, fruitful, multiply, replenish, subdue, and have dominion. These are the ingredients to start and build a Kingdom. This is what God had in mind when He created man male and female and placed them in earth suits (physical bodies). Is it safe to say God was Jesus in an earth suit? Please answer the question before going forward. Yes or no, what's your answer? If your answer is yes, let's move further. By answering yes, it should be safe to say Matthew 6:33 was God's word, "*Seek first the Kingdom of God and His righteousness.*"

It should be safe to read Matthew 4:17 "*From that time God began to preach and say repent for the Kingdom of Heaven is near.*" God said in Matthew 10:7, "*As you announce this, the Kingdom of Heaven has come near.*"

If you realize Adam didn't lose a religion, he lost dominion over the domain he was giving a Kingdom. Dom, (dom) as a noun, suffix dignity; office, realm; jurisdiction, state, or fact of being those having a (specific) office, occupation, interest, or character.

Adam simply lost a Kingdom for being disobedient to the will of God. Romans 5:17 *"For if, by the trespass of the one-man (Adam) death reigned through that one man (Adam), how much more will those who receive God's abundant provision of grace and the gift of righteousness reign (kingdom word) in life through the one man Jesus Christ (God)."*

We want to develop a mindset of "God said" or "God did" (God did it). Philippians 2:7 *But made Himself (God) nothing, taking the form of a servant born in men's likeness."*

John 10:30 *"I (Jesus) and the Father (God) are one."* Colossians 1:19 *"For in Him (Jesus) all the fullness of God was pleased to dwell."*

John 1:1 *"In the beginning was the Word, and the Word was God."*
So, when we read what Jesus said, we are reading what God said. So, saying that all God was talking

about is the Kingdom of God, the only message through Jesus. You can build your doctrine on what He did, such as His death, burial, and resurrection. The blood and these were means to the Kingdom. You can build your doctrine on Jesus, who was the door to the Kingdom. You can build your doctrine on what God taught through Jesus, or you can build your doctrine on the other books of the bible.

The book of Acts purposed to provide an account of that which Jesus continued to do through His church (ekklesia). Remember, earlier in the book, we explained that to have effective communication, you must have the same concept as when Jesus talked about Kingdom. The people understood the concept of a Kingdom because they were under a king in his Kingdom.

So, when we see the word 'Church' in the bible, the concept of this word "ekklesia" (ecclesia), the Greek word for church. Let us see what the concept of ekklesia was. Ekklesia is a political assembly of citizens of Ancient Greek states. It was the periodic meeting of the Athenian citizens for conducting public business and for considering affairs proposed by the council government meetings.

In 507 BC, the Athenians' leader, Cleisthenes, introduced a system of political reforms that he called 'Democratic' or ruled by the people. The system was made up of three separate institutions of the ekklesia; a government body that wrote the laws, the boule, and a council of representatives from the ten Athenian tribes. It was attended by males 19 years old and up. Meetings were held 40 times a year. The people understood the term ekklesia (church).

My late beautiful grandmother, Maggie Jackson, and I were talking on the phone. She asked me how I was doing, and my answer was, I'm chilling, her response was: are you cold? See, my grandmother did not understand the term chilling, so our communication was not effective because she did not understand the terms I was using. The book of Romans explains that salvation is offered through the gospel of Jesus Christ. (The gospel of the Kingdom). In the book of 1 Corinthians Apostle, Paul wrote to church members in Corinth to help them with their questions and problems and to strengthen the converts who struggled with reverting to their past beliefs and practices (it's hard to let go of what you've been taught since a child). 2 Corinthians was to express gratitude and strengthen the saints who had responded favorably to his previous letter. To warn of false teachers who corrupted the pure doctrines of Christ.

In the book of Galatians, Paul wrote a letter to the Galatians to counter the message of missionaries who had visited Galatia after he left. These missionaries taught that gentiles must follow parts of the Jewish law to be saved. These missionaries taught that Christian men had to accept the Jewish rite of circumcision.

The book of Ephesians explains how the church comes to full spiritual maturity in Christ. The first part describes the good news of what God has done. The second part gives instructions on how to live in light of those blessings. Ephesians ends with an encouragement to stand firm in the face of any hardship.

The book of Philippians was about hardship, humility, love, service, and hope beyond suffering in God's glory. The book of Colossians addresses problems in the church and challenges believers to examine their lives and be transformed through the love of Jesus. The book of 1 Thessalonians persuades the readers to live according to God's will. 2 Thessalonians addresses persecution, Jesus' return, and our need to remain faithful, reminding us that what we hope for shapes what we live for.

1 Timothy Paul teaches that Jesus Christ is the ransom for all and is our mediator with the Father. He instructs men and women on how to conduct themselves during worship. He outlines the qualification for bishops and deacons. To help the young church leader to better understand his duties. 2 Timothy emphasizes the power that comes from having a testimony of Jesus Christ. Contains prophecy of the perilous times that would exist.

The book of Titus, Paul's letter to Titus, urged him to remind Cretan believers that while they live in a sinful culture, they can be transformed into new humanity by the same grace that Jesus demonstrated when He died to redeem them. The book of Philemon demonstrates the gospel through action, it is written to Philemon,, whose slave Onesimus ran away and became a believer under Paul's teaching.

We see the writing of Apostle Paul deals with problems, corrections, comfort, church problems, thanks, gifts, and the gift of righteousness by faith. But we can see Paul's doctrine (teaching) found in Acts 28:30-31 *"And Paul dwelt two whole years in his own hired house, and received all that came in unto him, 31) preaching the Kingdom of God and teaching those things which concern the Lord Jesus Christ with all confidence no man forbidding him."*

Look at what Jesus said in Luke 4:*43*, *"And He said unto them, I MUST preach the Kingdom of God to other cities also for therefore am I sent."* Jesus told His disciples in Matthew 10:7, *"As you go, proclaim THIS message; the Kingdom of Heaven has come near."*

So, we see the original doctrine, preaching, and teaching was the Kingdom of God!! As pastors, leaders, and teachers, let's establish our doctrine on seeking first the Kingdom of God and His righteousness.

POWER COMES FROM CITIZENSHIP

To know your rights as a citizen of the United States is powerful. If you know your rights, this is sad to say; you can get away with murder as a citizen. 50% of people say OJ got away with murder. I was not there, so I do not know. Even though OJ was found not guilty, some evidence supports that he was guilty. Once the judge declares you not guilty, it does not matter what no one says.

John 10:10 *"The thief does not come except to steal, and to kill and to destroy if Satan can get you feeling depressed or condemned, he can steal, kill, or destroy you."*

If you do not know your rights, hire a great lawyer to get your joy back. As a citizen of the Kingdom of Heaven, we have joy. As a citizen of the United States, law enforcement works for you. Check this out; if you call the police, they will run red lights to get to your rescue because you got it like that as a citizen. We have the right to freedom of speech and expression. Right to a fair trial, right to free and Unperturbed Media, right to Vote Freely in public and open elections, Right to worship any religion in a free setting, and right to live permanently in the US.

As Citizens of the United States, we are blessed with a progressive government system that offers equal rights to all its legal citizens. The United States government grants certain rights to all its citizens. This is made possible by the United States Constitution, which is the highest law in America. The constitution guarantees that your rights are preserved and protected. The rights granted by the United States government must be respected. They also change from time to time, so keep a tab on the news and adjust your activities accordingly. These few rights we have seen work in our favor. It is good to be a citizen of the United States, especially compared to other countries.

Just take the time to ask yourself what rights I have as a citizen of the Kingdom of God. The first thing we know, to become a citizen of the United States, you must be born here then you access your rights.

And if you are not born here, the United States has a process that takes some time to receive permanent citizenship. We have a similar process in the Kingdom of God. We must also be born into the Kingdom of God, where Christ is the King, to become a citizen.

Luke 23:1-3 *"Then the whole multitude of them arose led Him to Pilate. 2) And they began to accuse Him, saying, "we found this fellow perverting the nation, and forbidding to pay taxes to Caesar, saying that He Himself is Christ, A king. 3) Then Pilate asked Him, saying, "Are You the king of the Jews?" He answered him and said, it is as you say."*

Apostle Paul talks about the gospel of Christ, the gospel meaning the good news. Christ, meaning the Anointed King. Romans 1:16-17 *"For I am not ashamed of the gospel of Christ; for it is the power of God unto salvation to everyone that believeth; to the Jews first, also to the Greek. 17) For therein is the righteousness of God revealed from faith to faith; as it is written, the just shall live by faith."* This scripture has put us in the right standing with the King of the Kingdom. We must explore our rights as Kingdom citizens.

Let's get a clear understanding of the word 'Rights.' Rights as a noun are having just claim to something by an individual. It can also be the claim to the inheritance of someone's Father's property or any other thing legally or constitutionally guaranteed to the person. Someone's rights cannot be denied if the person knows their rights. Most of us in the United States do not know our rights. We must attain an attorney and pay the attorney to exercise our rights as citizens. We also have rights as Kingdom citizens, but not many attorneys or Pastors can exercise our rights as Kingdom of Heaven citizens. That is why the devil gets away with murder! Because we do not understand our Heavenly Rights.

You have the right to be delivered, you have the right to be healed, you have the right to be prosperous, and you have the right to be whole. We have the right to be the righteousness of God in Christ Jesus. We are in right standing with God and the country of Heaven. Philippians 3:20 *"But our citizenship is in Heaven. And we eagerly await a Savior from there, the Lord Jesus Christ."* We have Heavenly rights as born-again citizens.

1 Peter 2:24 *"Who His own self bares our sins in His own body on the tree, that we being dead to sin, should live unto righteousness by whose stripes you were healed."*

We have the right to be healed because our healing has been paid for by the stripes of Jesus, our righteousness, paid for by the blood of Jesus!

Just before we were born in the United States, we as African-Americans had to fight for our Civil Rights. You must know what your rights are. Fight for what is yours. We have the right to be Kingdom Citizens. We must know and fight for our Rights as kingdom citizens. This is something serious. You must understand you have to fight to keep the understanding of the Kingdom. Because Matthew 13:19 Says when anyone hears the word of the Kingdom and does not understand it, then the wicked one comes and snatches away what was sown in his heart. This is he who received seed by the wayside.

Ephesians 6:11-12 *"Put on the whole armor of God that you may be able to stand against the wiles of the devil. For we do not wrestle against flesh and blood, but against principalities, against powers, against the ruler of the darkness of this age, against spiritual hosts of wickedness in heavenly places."*

We really must receive and protect the word of the Kingdom so we can experience this Kingdom life that Jesus paid for in full for us to have. This word

'Against' was used in these previous verses we just read seven times to show us we are in a fight. Understand these forces attacks the headquarters, which is your mind, the center of everything.

<u>Against</u> is defined as in opposition or hostility to, as a defense or protection. As we get deeper into understanding the Kingdom. Know that you will experience some resistance, and it will appear that it will be coming within you, from your own thinking, press through it. If you press through what you have been taught about membership, you can learn about citizenship. You do not have to be upset when the Pastor doesn't come to see his members in a time of need, as a citizen who knows their rights can handle any situation. You must press through religious teaching. Jesus did say to repent simply means changing the way you think because I'm about to introduce the Kingdom of God to you! You must be willing to change the way you think. Welcome to the Kingdom!!

Romans 14:17 *"For the Kingdom of God is not a matter of what we eat or drink, but of living a life of goodness and peace and joy in the Holy Spirit. Who could use some goodness, peace, and joy in the Holy Spirit?*

1 Corinthians 4:*20 "For the Kingdom of God is not in word, but in Power."* Jesus tells His disciples in Luke 10:19 *"Behold, I give unto you power to tread on serpents and scorpions, and over all the power of the enemy, and nothing shall by any means hurt you."* Let us stop for a second and recap, and we see joy, peace, goodness, and power associated with the Kingdom of God. This is the culture of the Kingdom of God. If you are having difficulty with living in power over every circumstance with joy, peace, and goodness.

My air conditioner went out this summer, our inside unit and outside unit; because I had the power (Money) to solve the problem, my joy and peace were kept. That's power! Jesus brings clarity in Matthew 6:*10 "Thy Kingdom come, thy will be done in earth, as it is in Heaven."* Jesus was saying let the culture of Heaven come to the earth.

Merriam-Webster defines culture as the set of shared attitudes, values, goals, and practices that characterizes an institution or organization. The act of developing intellectual and moral faculties, especially by education. The integrated pattern of human knowledge, belief, and behavior depends upon the capacity for learning and transmitting knowledge to succeeding generations.

A small example of culture let us compare the fastfood restaurant Chick-fil-a vs. Mcdonalds' two different atmospheres, two different cultures. Chickfil-a has been trained differently than most fastfood restaurants, period. They seem to never get your order wrong; Chick-fil-a cares about their employees. They are available everywhere, and employees have the utmost attitude wherever you visit them.

Another example is that Jesus' disciples were disciplined differently, all they ever heard Jesus teach was the Kingdom. The third example is a couple who can be married for 30 years and do everything together, then one person meets Jesus, and their whole lifestyle changes and the two who had everything in common are now so different. Now the difference will depend on did they meet Jesus, who taught the Kingdom, or their denominational teaching? Because it will determine how you talk, how you dress, and ultimately how you live.

The Jesus in the bible is totally different from the people we meet today and say they met Jesus. Because they established a religion that produces rituals which are a series of actions or behavior regularly and invariably followed by someone. Jesus did not, I mean, never bought a religion; he brought the Kingdom and its culture. Jesus was different from the religious people in His days and the religious people in our days. If your ministry is not established on the message Jesus taught, which was the Kingdom of God, it was not the blood, it was not being born again, it was not the resurrection.

All these acts were means for us to enter the Kingdom, but it was not the Kingdom's message. The Kingdom brings amazement. Matthew 7:28-29 *"When Jesus finished these words, the crowd were amazed at His teaching, for He was teaching them as one having authority and not as their scribes."* Scribes were religious leaders in Jesus's days who cosigned for Jesus' crucifixion. Matthew 13:54 *"He came to His hometown and began teaching them in their synagogue so that they were astonished and said where did this man get this wisdom and these miraculous powers."*

Kingdom vs. Religion. Kingdom trumps religion every day all day. The culture of the Kingdom Jesus brought to the earth was a culture of power that He introduced to Chick-fil-a Lol, I mean His disciples. Mark 1:27 *"And they were all amazed, insomuch that they questioned among themselves, saying, what thing is this? What new doctrine (teaching) is this? For with authority commanded He even the unclean spirits, and they do obey Him."*

Let's answer the question which was asked what thing is this? What new teaching is this? Let's start from verse one of Mark chapter 1, which reads, *"The beginning of the gospel of Jesus Christ, the Son of God 2) as it is written in the prophets, behold I send my messenger before thy face, which shall prepare the way before thee. 3) the voice of one crying in the wilderness, prepare ye the way of the Lord, make His paths straight. 4) John did baptize in the wilderness and preached the baptism of repentance for the remission of sin."*

Let us cross-reference to establish John's mission on Jesus' behalf in Matthew 3:*1-2* *"In those days came John the Baptist preaching in the wilderness of Judea 2) and saying, repent ye for the Kingdom of Heaven is at hand."*

Let us go back to Mark to answer the two questions in verse 27-chapter 1: What is this? What new teaching is this? Here is the answer Mark 1:14-*15* *"Now after John was put in prison. Jesus came into Galilee, preaching the gospel of the Kingdom of God. 15) And saying the time is fulfilled, and the Kingdom of God is at hand repent ye and believe the gospel!!"*

PRAYER OF SALVATION

Say this prayer:

Lord Jesus, you are the Son of God, and You died on the cross for my sins.

And now You are alive with all power, and I receive You as my Lord and Savior.

Take my life and allow me to manifest Your will on earth as it is in Heaven.

Thy Kingdom come, Thy Government come,

Thy culture comes, and Thy value system comes to earth now.

Thy Will, intention, purpose, and constitution be done on earth as it is in Heaven.

Heavenly Father, colonize me now!

REFERENCES

New King James, Thomas Nelson Publisher

Rediscovering The Kingdom, Myles Munroe

ABOUT THE AUTHOR

Sidney Sawyer III's impressive assignment is to re-present God to a world that has seen Him through the eyes of religion and not through the eyes of The Kingdom of God and to let them know that He has an impressive plan for their lives. God has called Sidney to be a teacher, and he brings revelation, knowledge, and practical insight to the Body of Christ with his methods of teaching. Sidney serves in ministry with his awesome wife, Kelita Sawyer, under the leadership of Apostle Ernest Gwinn III and Prophetess Linda Gwinn at The Church of Glory. He is also a Sales Consultant at Springhill Toyota. He has an awesome daughter & son, Symone MeKayla Sawyer and Sidney Sawyer IV. He also authors three other books; *The BluePrint of Faith*, *Moving From Potential To Purpose*, and *Your New Identity Design To Win*, which are available at Amazon and SidneySawyer.org

Made in the USA
Middletown, DE
04 December 2022